A Gift For

"" *Jody* ""

..................*Jody*..................

Love
From

.......*Mom + Dad*.......

"*L*"

I nag because
I love.

Copyright © 2009
Hallmark Licensing, Inc.

Published by Hallmark Books,
a division of Hallmark Cards, Inc.,
Kansas City, MO 64141
Visit us on the Web at
www.Hallmark.com.

Editorial Director: Todd Hafer
Editors: Megan Langford
and Theresa Trinder
Art Director: Kevin Swanson
Designer: Mary Eakin
Production Artist: Dan Horton

Contributing Writers:
Keely Chace, Chris Conti,
Renee Daniels, Russ Ediger,
Jennifer Fujita, Jake Gahr,
Bill Gray, Megan Haave,
Mark Oatman, Cat Skorupski,
Dee Ann Stewart, Dan Taylor,
and Myra Zirkle

ISBN: 978-1-59530-027-0
BOK4347

Because I Said So!

MODERN MOMS TELL IT LIKE IT IS

Now listen, Mommy needs
some time to drink—
I mean, think—
so you go to sleep now, OK?

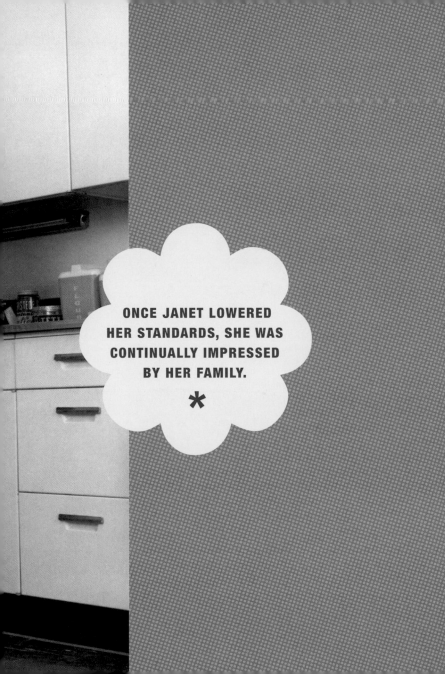

ONCE JANET LOWERED
HER STANDARDS, SHE WAS
CONTINUALLY IMPRESSED
BY HER FAMILY.

*

Whoever cares at all about my happiness and possible heart condition will come in for supper right now!

EVERYTHING'S BETTER
WITH A LITTLE DASH
OF GUILT.

*

The most important part of
my beauty routine? A deadbolt
on the bathroom door.

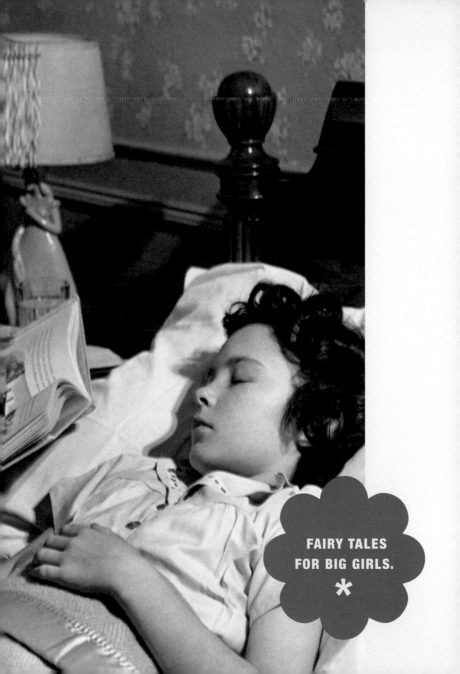

FAIRY TALES
FOR BIG GIRLS.

*

PAM LEFT NO
QUESTION AS TO
WHO WOULD WIN THE
"MY MOM'S BETTER THAN
YOUR MOM" DEBATE.

If you think
I dry DISHES fast,
you should see the magic
I can work with tears.

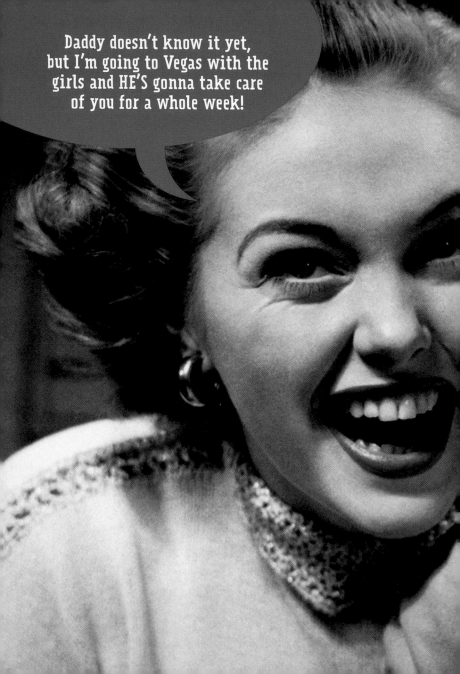

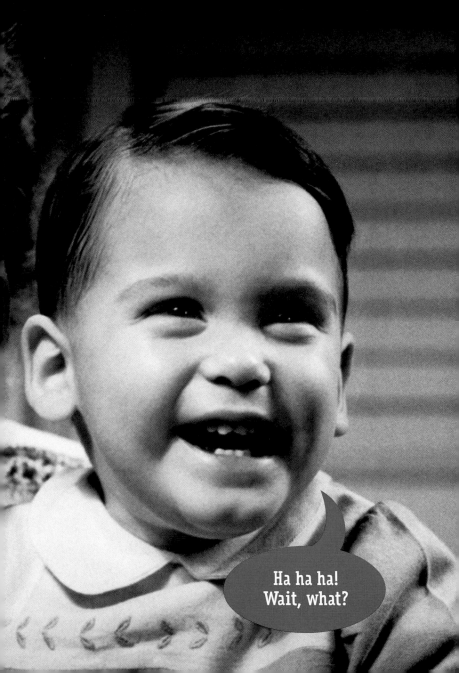

Ha ha ha!
Wait, what?

PRETTY MUCH ALL
THEY DO IS EAT AND SLEEP.
SAME THING GOES
FOR BABIES, TOO.

*

Bet Starbucks can't make a cup like this.

JEAN WAS FAMOUS
FOR HER
"COFFEE WITH A KICK."

And my calculations
indicate that it's just
over three million.

A TYPICAL MOM
ESTIMATES HER "IF I HAD
A NICKEL" EARNINGS.

FOR THE PERFECT GETAWAY, PACK PLENTY OF SNACKS, SOME MAGAZINES, AND EXTRA UNDERWEAR. HUSBAND AND KIDS OPTIONAL.

*

Oh, boo hoo.
Try being in labor
for twenty-seven hours.

It doesn't say a darn thing
about a stork . . . unless,
maybe that's supposed
to be his beak?

No, my mom's the best!

CASUALTIES OF THE
ENSUING FIGHT INCLUDED
ONE TOOTH, A SWEATER,
AND AN OVERDUE
LIBRARY BOOK.

Of course I love my family!
That's the thing that keeps me
from killing them!

A SUPPORTIVE MOM
GIVES US THE TOOLS
WE NEED TO SUCCEED.

*

COLLEEN DIDN'T KNOW
WHETHER TO PUNISH HER
OR COMMEND HER ON SUCH
A WELL-CRAFTED LIE.

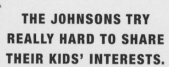

THE JOHNSONS TRY
REALLY HARD TO SHARE
THEIR KIDS' INTERESTS.

SHE ALWAYS TOLD
HER KIDS THAT IT WAS
HER JOB TO EMBARRASS THEM.
THEY JUST DIDN'T KNOW
THE JOB CAME
WITH A UNIFORM.

Don't worry, Mom.
We're gonna catch dinner
with our bare hands!

MOM KNOWS THAT
HAVING THE PIZZA PLACE
ON SPEED DIAL IS ALWAYS
A GOOD IDEA.

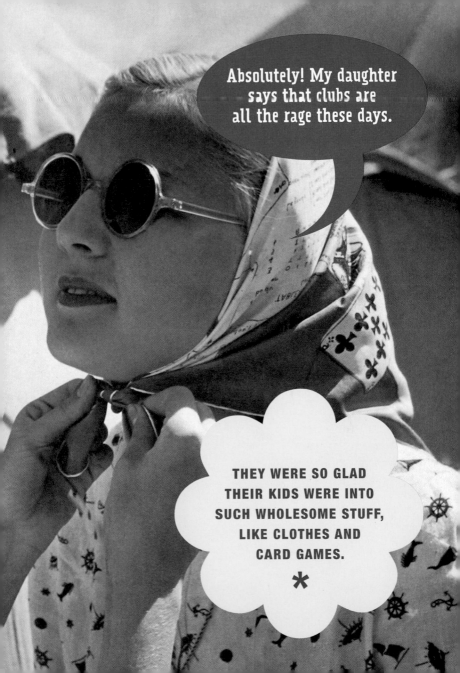

Dang it, Larry!
How did you get the remote
in there, anyway?

You never know.

MOMS ARE NEVER
CAUGHT UNPREPARED.

MARRIAGE LESSON
#24.

*

She has no idea
what I'm about to do
in my pants.

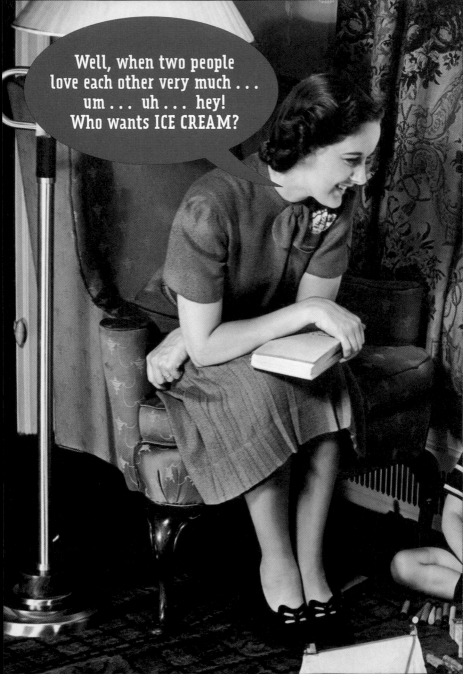

ONLY MOM KNOWS HOW TO HANDLE THE REALLY BIG QUESTIONS.

*

YOU DON'T EXACTLY NEED
DNA TESTING TO SEE WHEN
THE SHEER PERFECTION GENE
HAS BEEN SUCCESSFULLY
PASSED ON.

Twizzlers, a twelve-pack of Dr. Pepper, and a pony? Yeah, right.

WHEN KIDS ADD TO THE SHOPPING LIST.

A GOOD MOM
ALWAYS PRACTICES
QUALITY CONTROL.

*

Dear God, please tell my mom that "everyone else is doing it" is TOO a good enough reason.

I'll show everybody that moms aren't the only ones who know how to fry soup!

If you have a problem meringue can't solve, you're not using enough of it.

With the right amount of fumes, even housekeeping isn't so bad!

Are you going to
teach him to leave the hairs
in the sink, too?

Just remember,
you're the smartest, nicest,
bravest, prettiest, funniest . . .
hey, get back here,
I'm not finished!

Oh, drat! I've left the keys to the yacht in the Maserati again!

WHEN ALL PEG SAW WERE EMPTY GUM WRAPPERS AND USED TISSUES, SELF-DELUSION GOT HER THROUGH THE DAY.

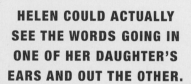

HELEN COULD ACTUALLY
SEE THE WORDS GOING IN
ONE OF HER DAUGHTER'S
EARS AND OUT THE OTHER.

Mmmm . . .
Bran Buddies!

A MOM IS A FRIEND
WHO KEEPS YOU IN THE DARK
ABOUT SUGAR CEREALS
AS LONG AS SHE CAN.

You can do it, honey!
Good job!
Get that thingy!

MOM ALWAYS CHEERS,
EVEN WHEN SHE HAS
NO IDEA WHAT'S GOING ON.

Moms, we want to hear you tell it like it is.
If you enjoyed this book, drop us a line!

Please send your comments to:
Hallmark Book Feedback
P.O. Box 419034
Mail Drop 215
Kansas City, Missouri 64141

Or e-mail us at:
booknotes@hallmark.com